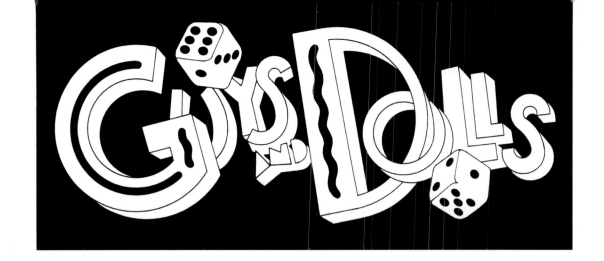

Back Cover photo courtesy of Martha Swope

ISBN 978-0-7935-2872-1

Applications for performance of this work, whether legitimate, stock, amateur, or foreign, should be addressed to:

MUSIC THEATRE INTERNATIONAL
545 8th Avenue
New York, NY 10018
(212) 868-6668

http://www.mplcommunications.com

HAL•LEONARD®
CORPORATION
7777 W. BLUEMOUND RD. P.O. BOX 13819 MILWAUKEE, WI 53213

CONTENTS

FUGUE FOR TINHORNS

By FRANK LOESSER

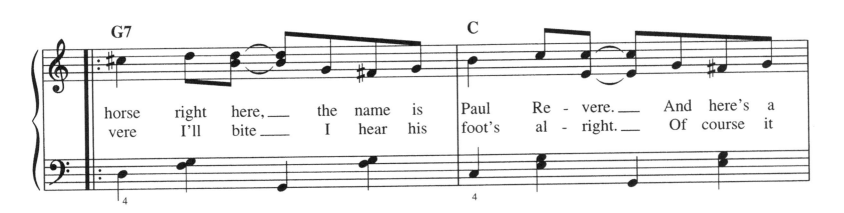

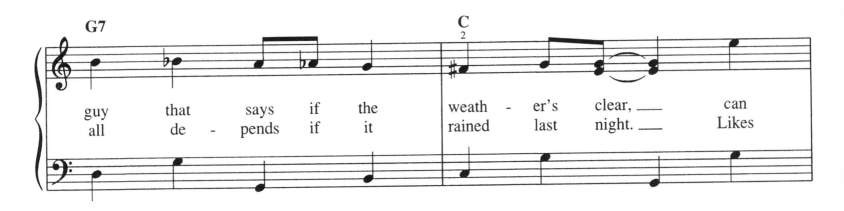

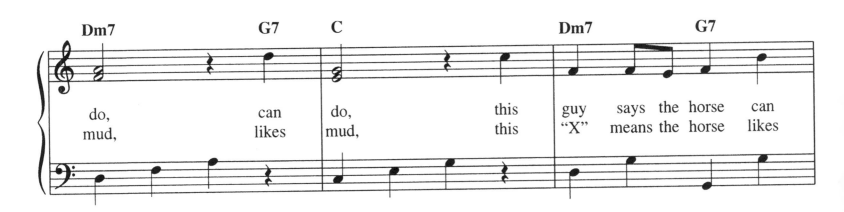

6

I'LL KNOW

By FRANK LOESSER

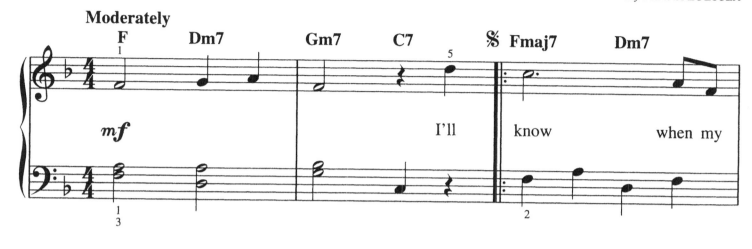

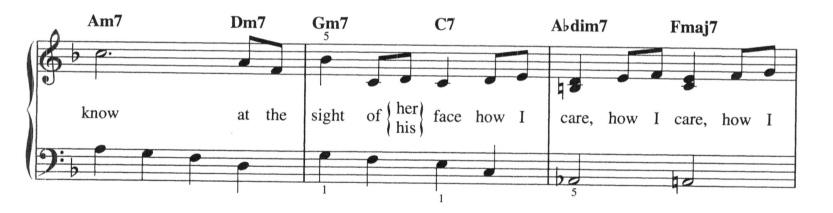

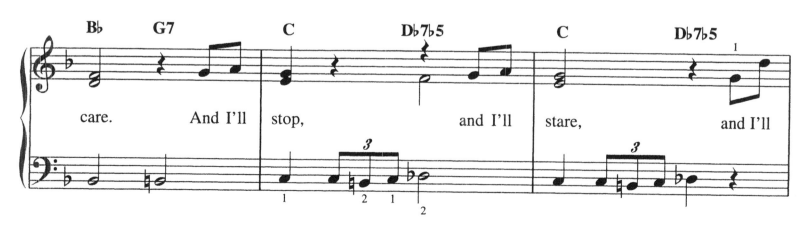

know   long be - fore   we can speak, I'll   know   in my

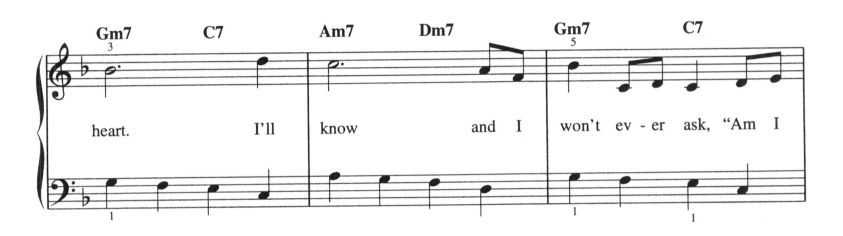

heart.   I'll   know   and I   won't ev - er ask, "Am I

right, am I wise, am I   smart?"   But I'll   stop   and I'll

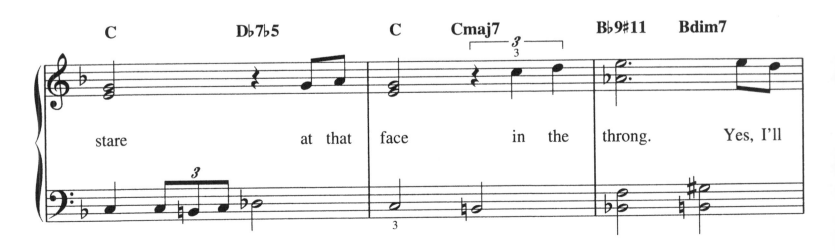

stare   at that   face   in the   throng.   Yes, I'll

A BUSHEL AND A PECK

By FRANK LOESSER

a- bout you

'Cause

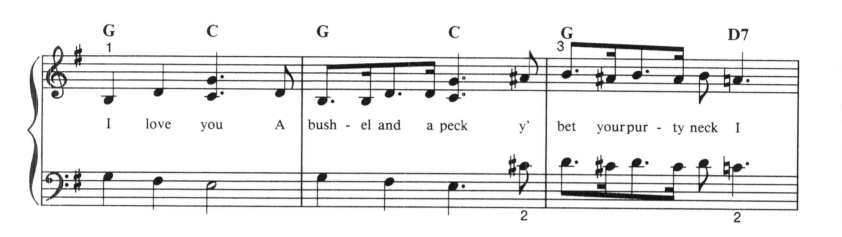

I love you A bush - el and a peck y' bet your pur - ty neck I

do

Doo - dle oo - dle oo - dle

Doo - dle oo - dle oo - dle

Doo - dle oo - dle oo - dle

ooo.

ooo.

ADELAIDE'S LAMENT

By FRANK LOESSER

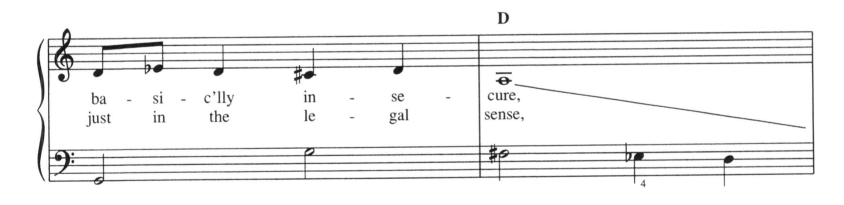

av' - rage un - mar - ried fe - male,
fe - male re - main - ing sin - gle,

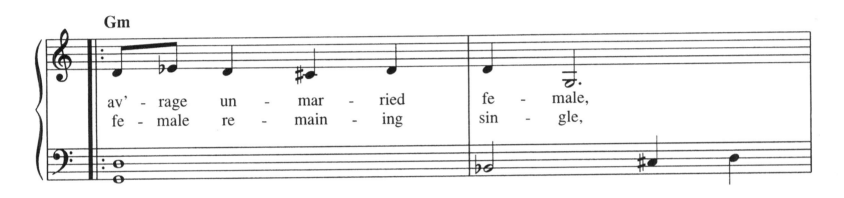

ba - si - c'lly in - se - cure,
just in the le - gal sense,

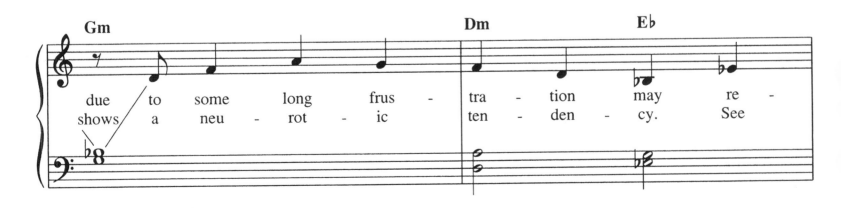

due to some long frus - tra - tion may re -
shows a neu - rot - ic ten - den - cy. See

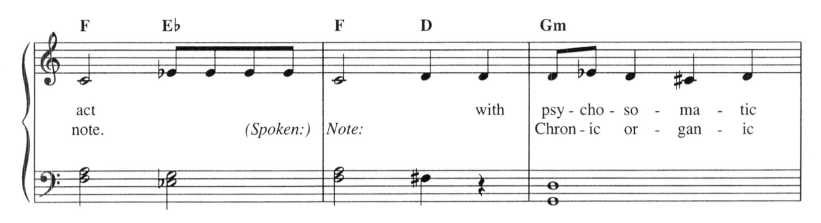

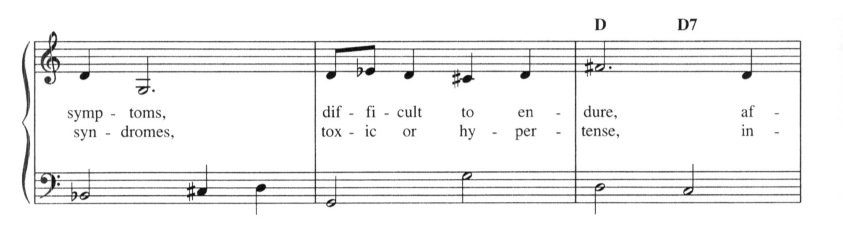

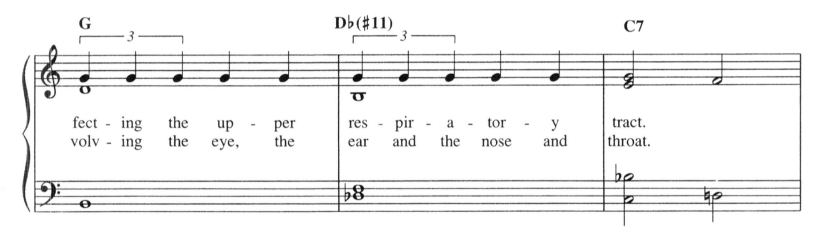

14

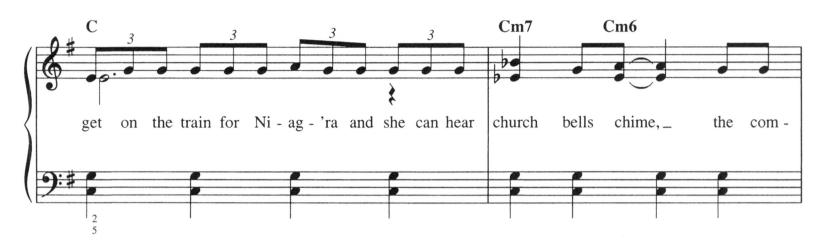

get on the train for Ni - ag - 'ra and she can hear church bells chime, __ the com -

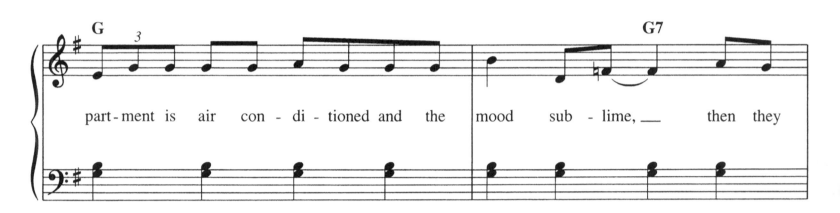

part - ment is air con - di - tioned and the mood sub - lime, ___ then they

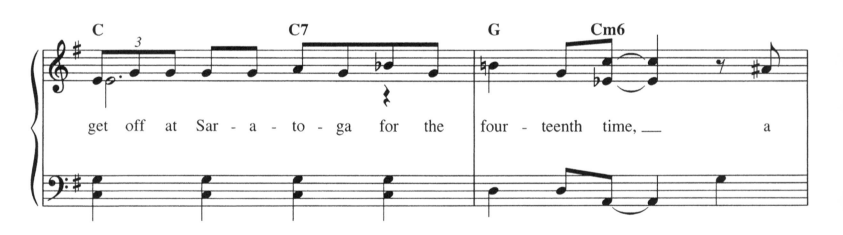

get off at Sar - a - to - ga for the four - teenth time, ___ a

per - son ___ can de - vel - op La grippe (Hm) La grippe, La

post   na - sal drip,   with the   wheez - es   and   the   sneez - es   and a

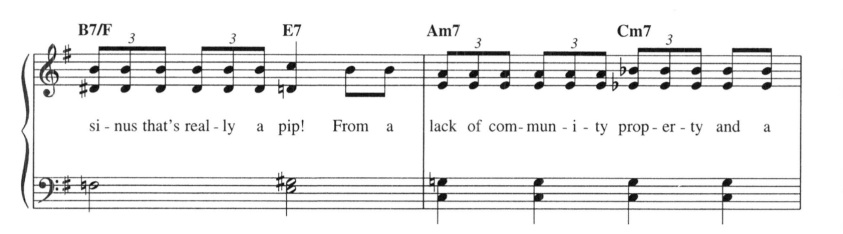

si - nus that's real - ly a pip! From a   lack of com - mun - i - ty prop - er - ty and a

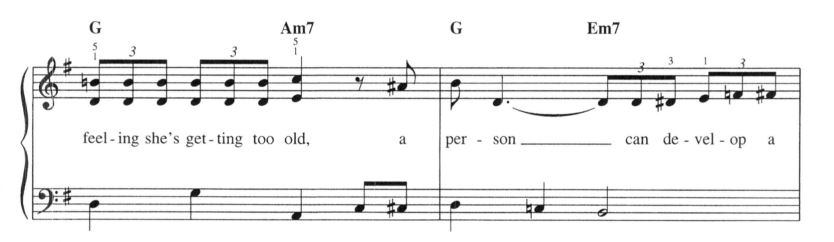

feel - ing she's get - ting too old,   a   per - son _____ can de - vel - op a

bad,   bad   cold.

GUYS AND DOLLS

By FRANK LOESSER

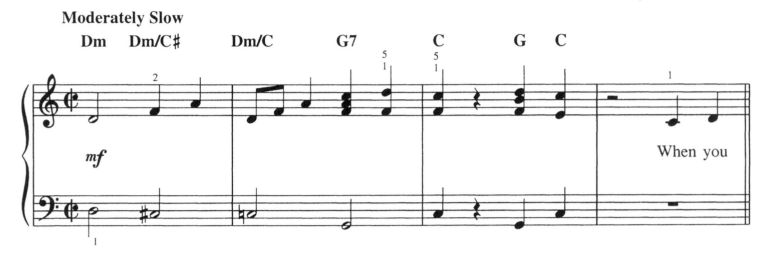

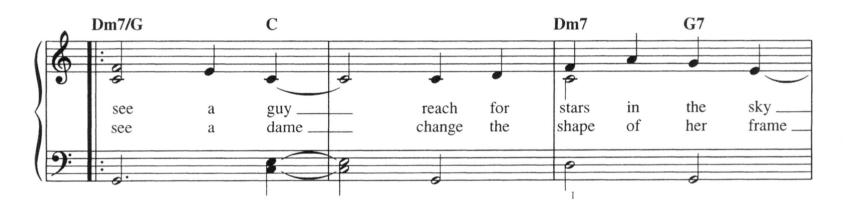

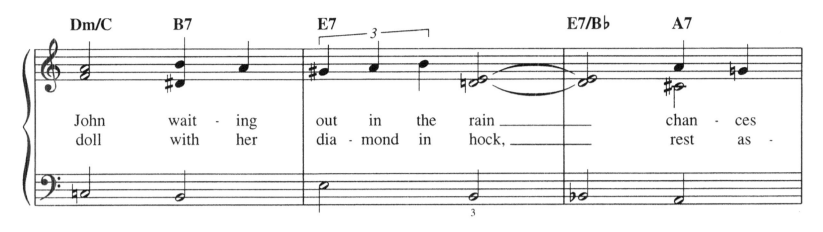

John wait - ing out in the rain _____ chan - ces
doll with her dia - mond in hock, _____ rest as -

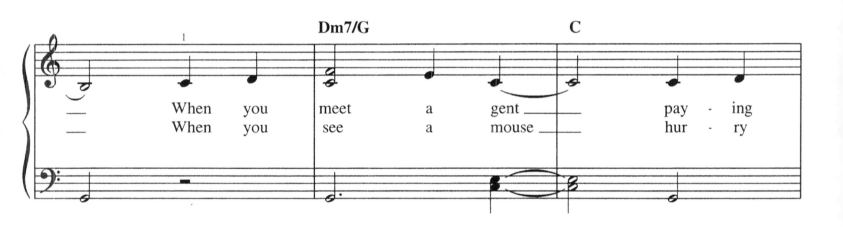

are he's in - sane as on - ly a John can be for a Jane. ____
sured that the rock as gone to re - stock some gen - tle - man jock. ____

When you meet a gent _____ pay - ing
When you see a mouse _____ hur - ry

all kinds of rent _____ for a flat that could
out of the house _____ and she runs twen - ty

flat - ten the Taj Ma - hal, _____ call it
blocks for ci - gars and rye, _____ call it

sad, call it fun - ny, but it's bet - ter than e - ven
dumb, call it clev - er, ah, but you can give odds for -

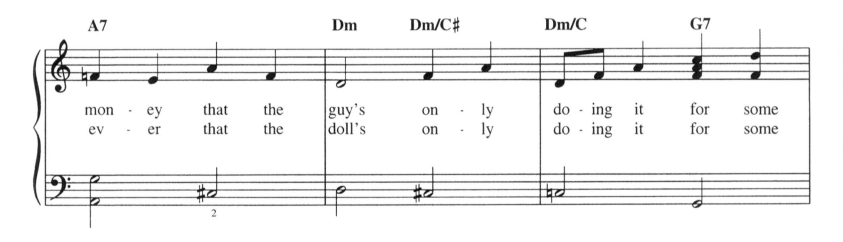

mon - ey that the guy's on - ly do - ing it for some
ev - er that the doll's on - ly do - ing it for some

doll. On the oth-er hand: when you guy.

I'VE NEVER BEEN IN LOVE BEFORE

By FRANK LOESSER

been in love be - fore.   I   thought my heart was

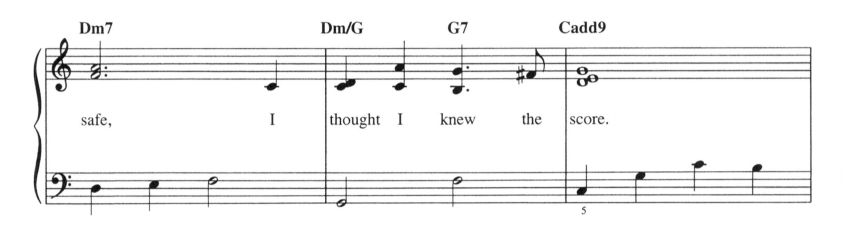

safe,   I   thought I   knew the   score.

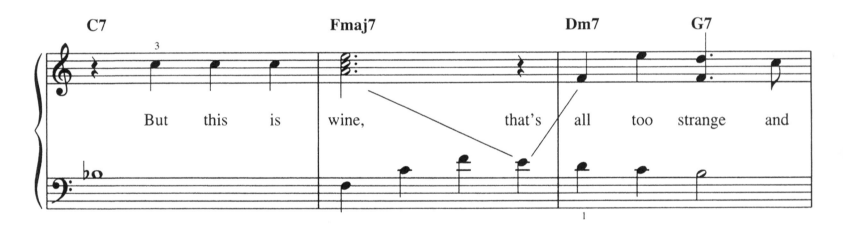

But   this   is   wine,   that's   all   too   strange   and

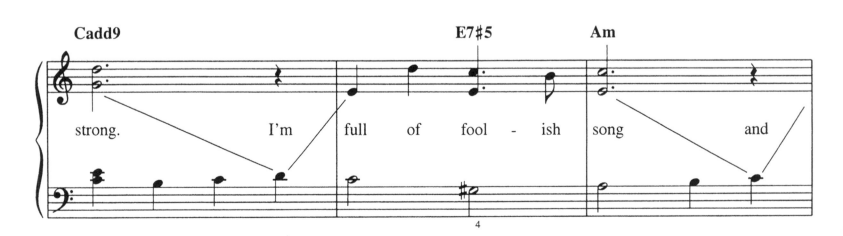

strong.   I'm   full   of   fool - ish   song   and

IF I WERE A BELL

By FRANK LOESSER

Medium Bounce

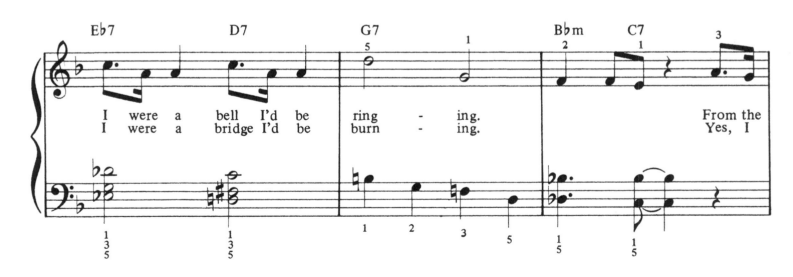

TAKE BACK YOUR MINK

By FRANK LOESSER

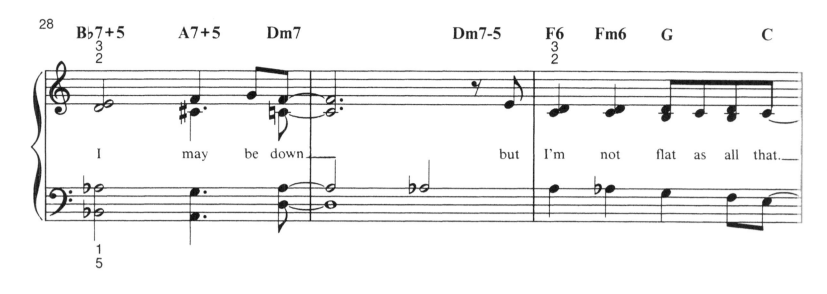

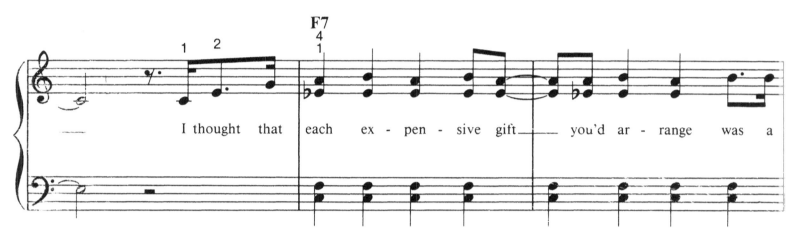

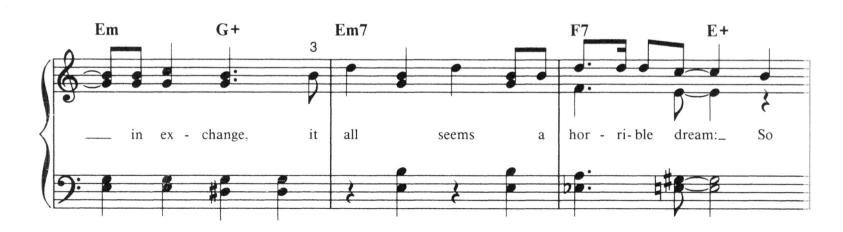

Take back your mink___ These old worn out pelts___

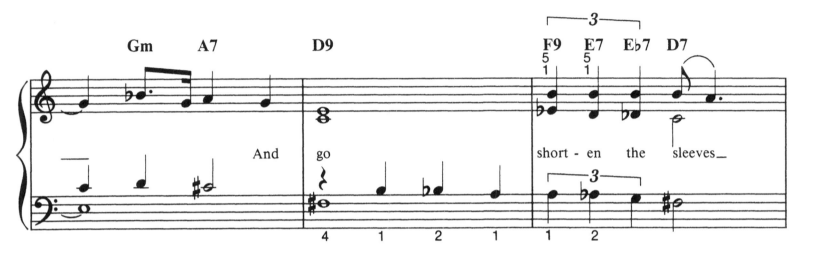

___ And go short - en the sleeves___

For some - bod - y else!___ *f*

MORE I CANNOT WISH YOU

By FRANK LOESSER

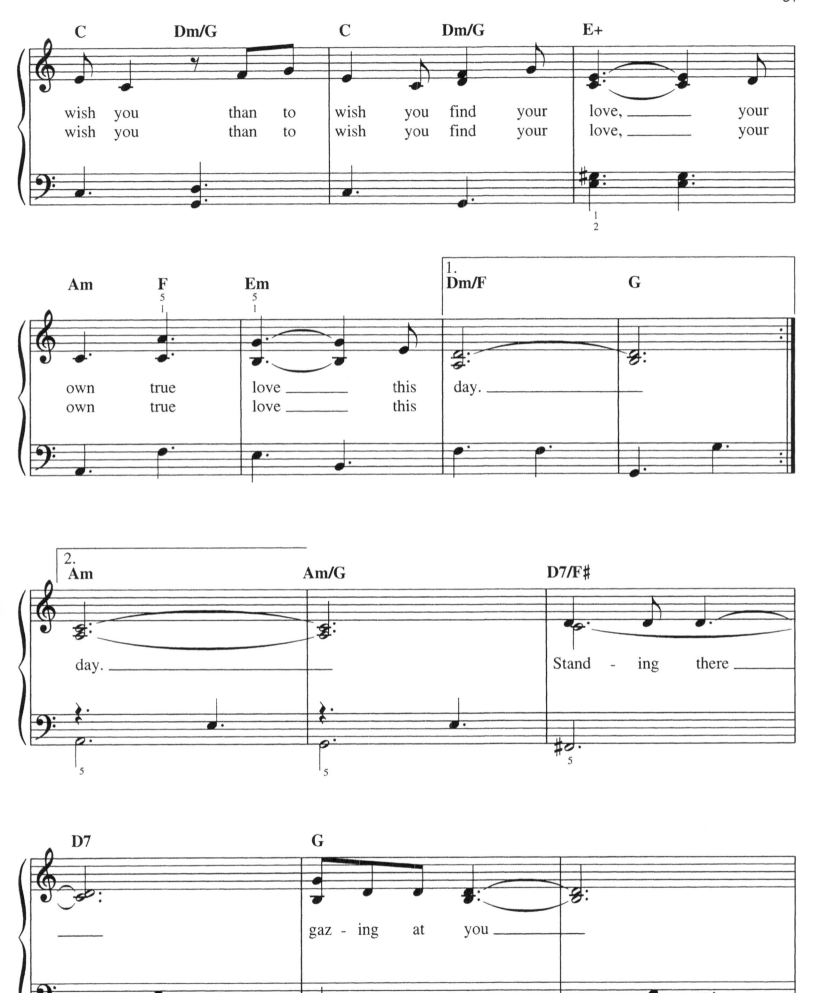

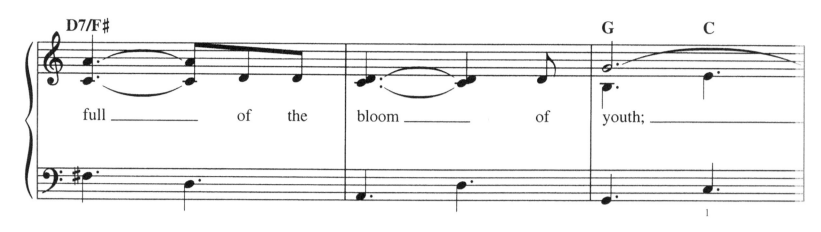

full _____ of the bloom _____ of youth; _____

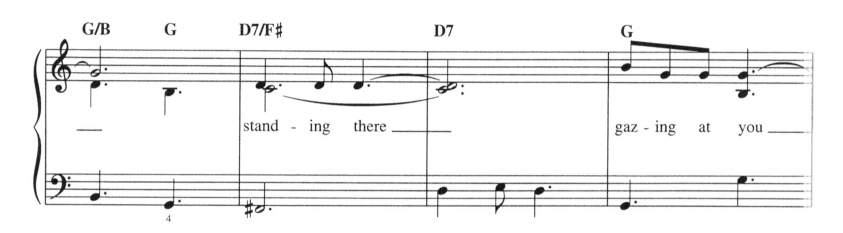

__ stand - ing there _____ gaz - ing at you _____

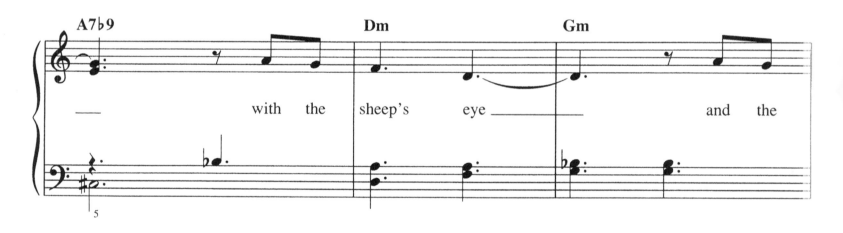

__ with the sheep's eye _____ and the

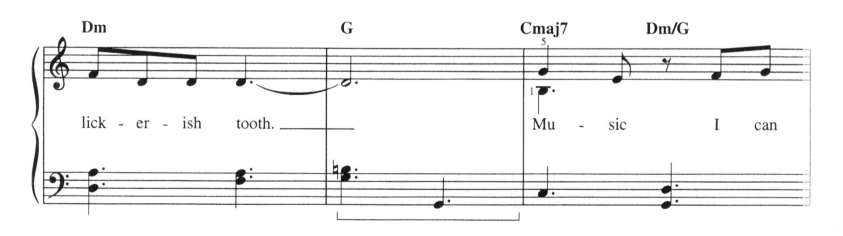

lick - er - ish tooth. _____ Mu - sic I can

33

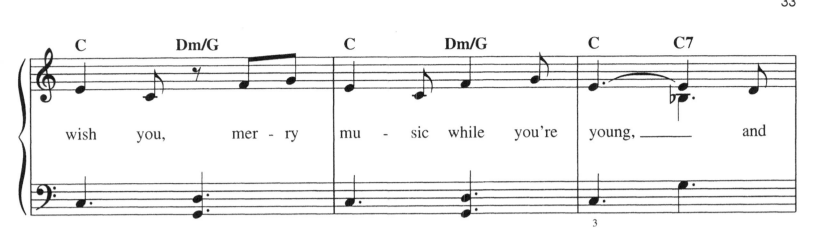

wish you, mer - ry mu - sic while you're young, _____ and

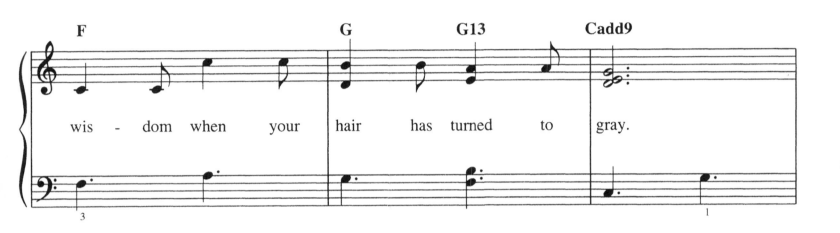

wis - dom when your hair has turned to gray.

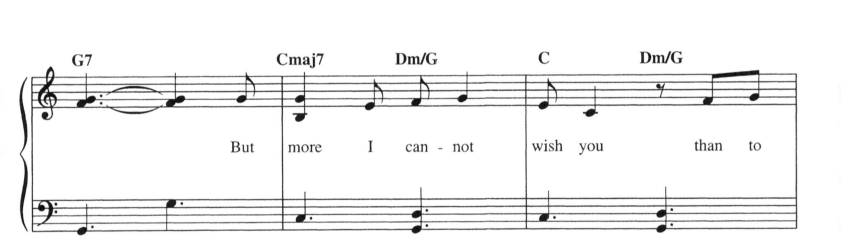

But more I can - not wish you than to

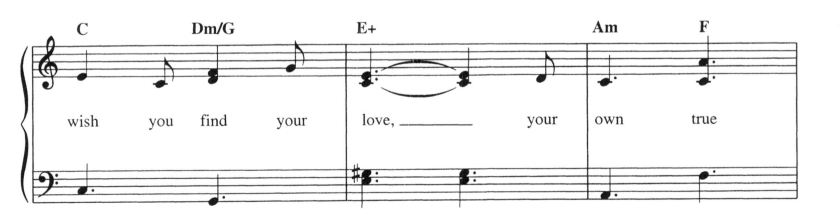

wish you find your love, _____ your own true

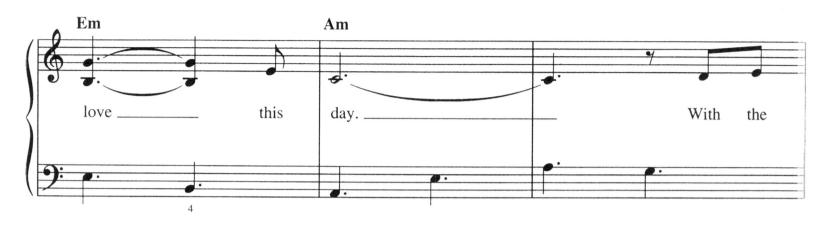

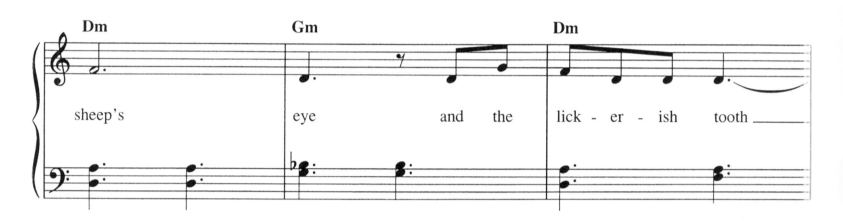

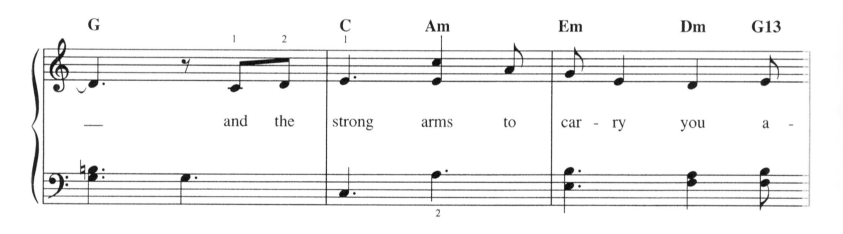

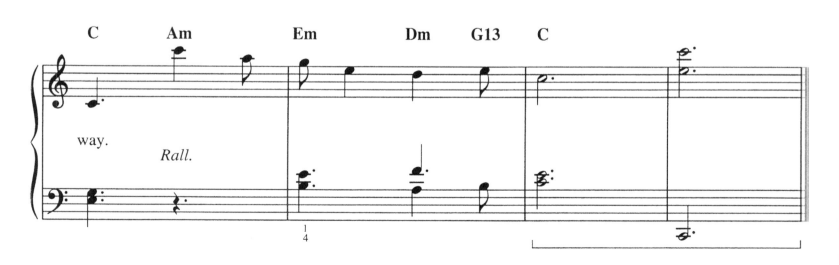

SUE ME

By FRANK LOESSER

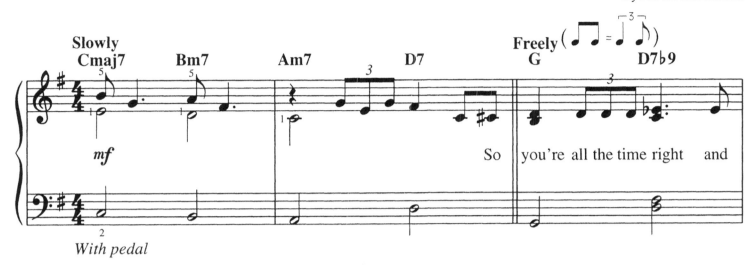

So you're all the time right and

I'm all the time wrong, so my char-ac-ter's weak and

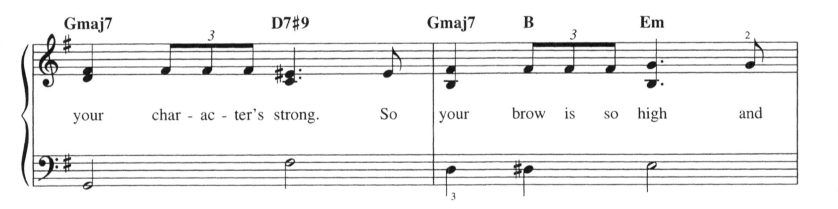

your char-ac-ter's strong. So your brow is so high and

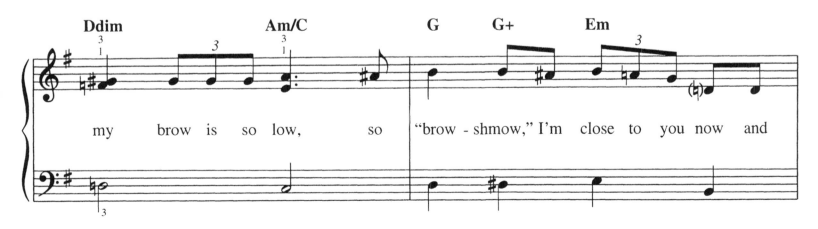

my brow is so low, so "brow-shmow," I'm close to you now and

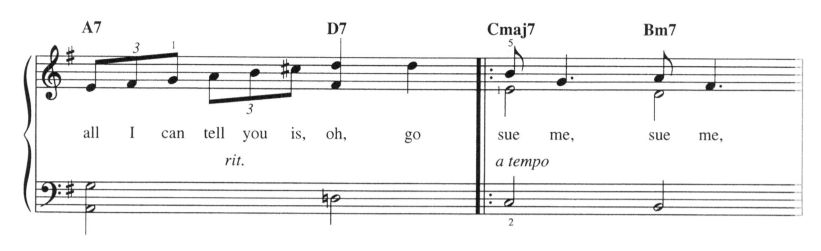

all I can tell you is, oh, go sue me, sue me,

rit.   *a tempo*

what can you do me? I love you.

Give a hol-ler and hate me, hate me

go a-head hate me, I love you.   All

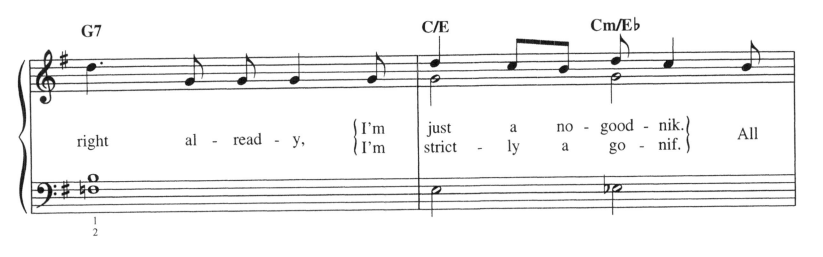

right al - read - y, { I'm just a no - good - nik. / I'm strict - ly a go - nif. } All

right al - read - y, it's true, so Nu? So

sue me, sue me, what can you do me?

I love you. you.
rit.

LUCK BE A LADY

By FRANK LOESSER

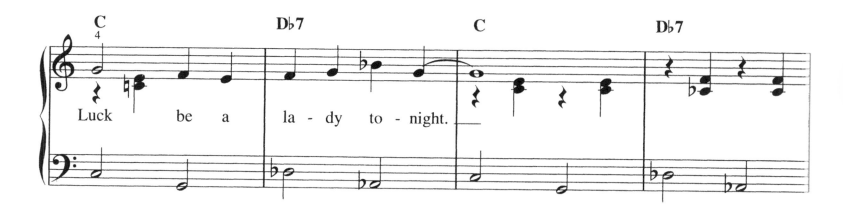

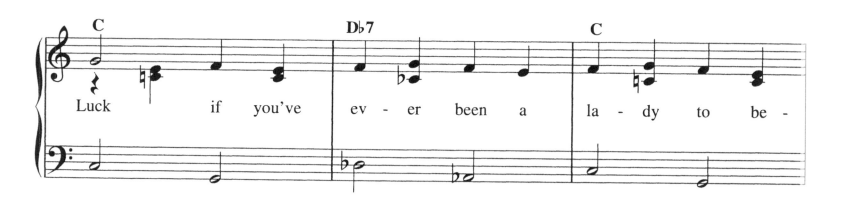

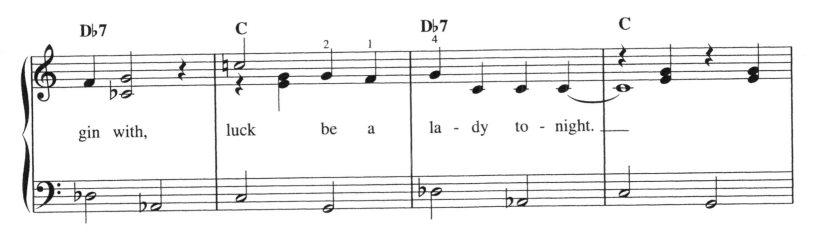

gin with, luck be a la - dy to - night.

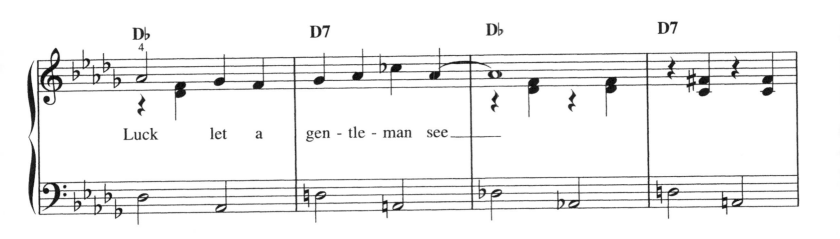

Luck let a gen - tle - man see

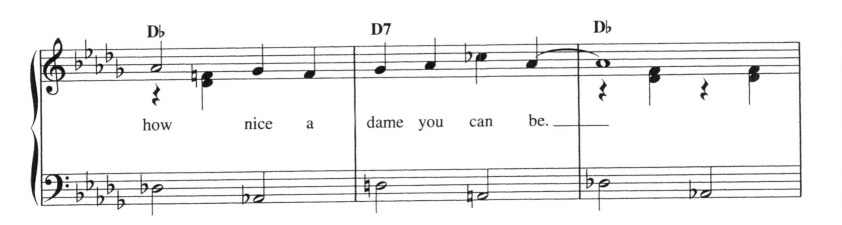

how nice a dame you can be.

40

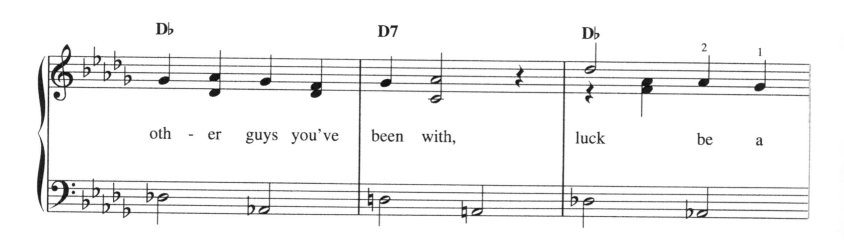

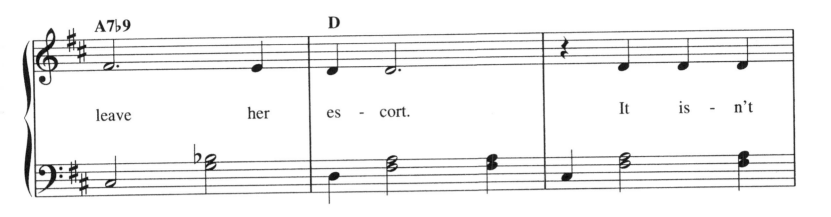

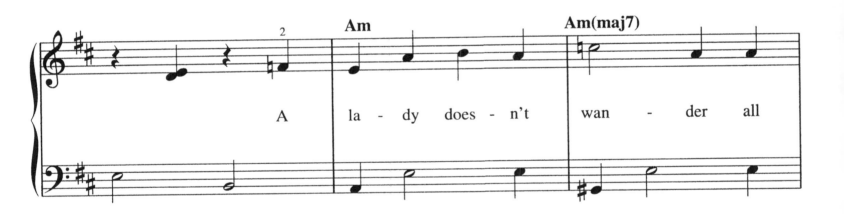

41

42

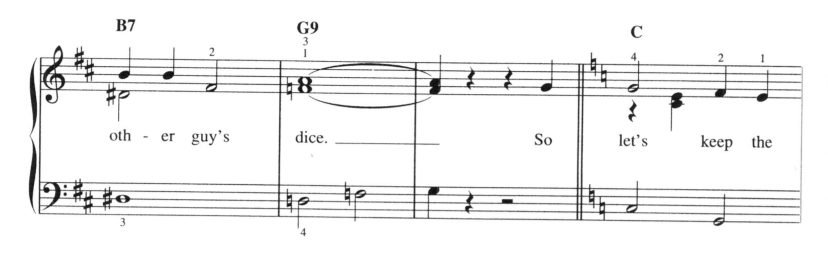

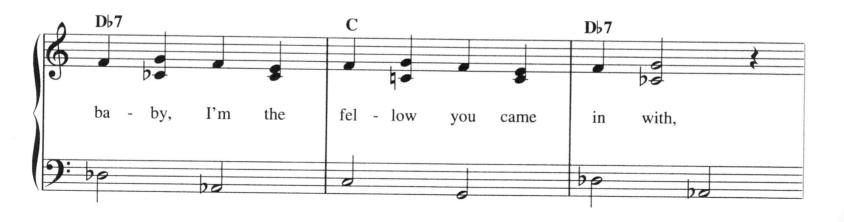

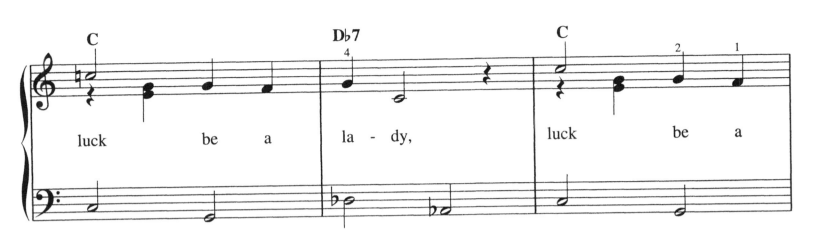

luck be a la - dy, luck be a

la - dy, luck be a la - dy to - night.

SIT DOWN YOU'RE ROCKIN' THE BOAT

By FRANK LOESSER

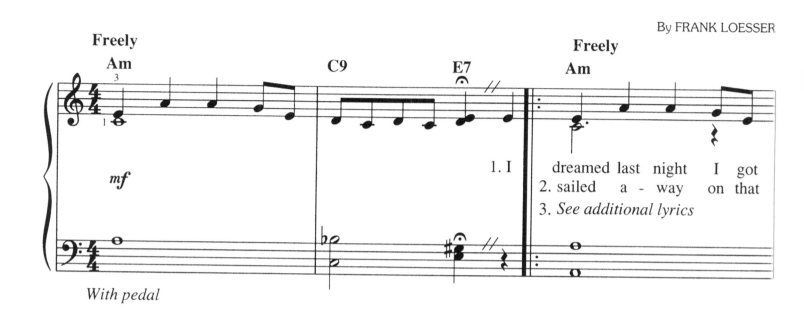

1. I dreamed last night I got
2. sailed a - way on that
3. *See additional lyrics*

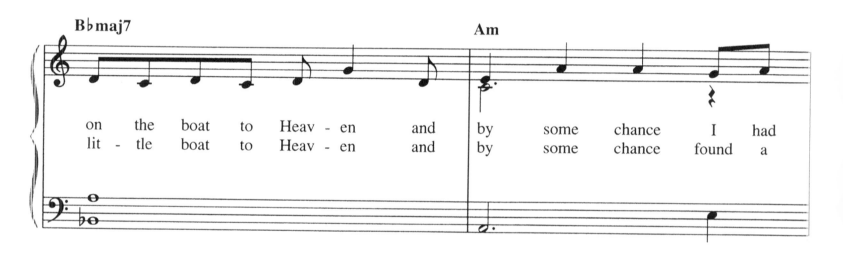

on the boat to Heav - en and by some chance I had
lit - tle boat to Heav - en and by some chance found a

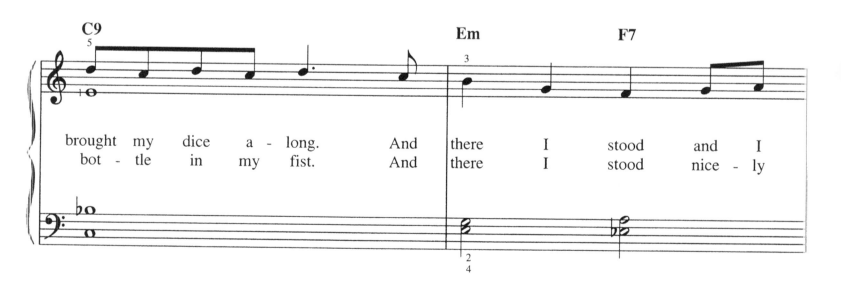

brought my dice a - long. And there I stood and I
bot - tle in my fist. And there I stood nice - ly

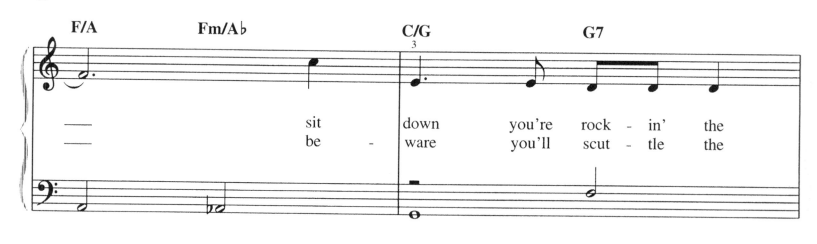

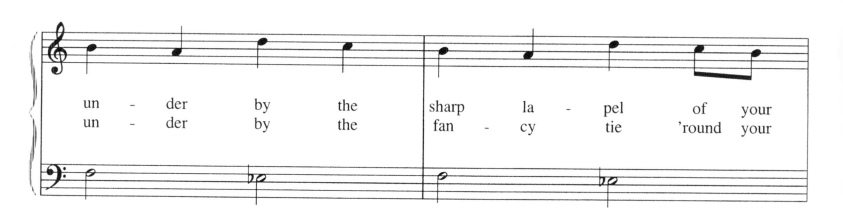

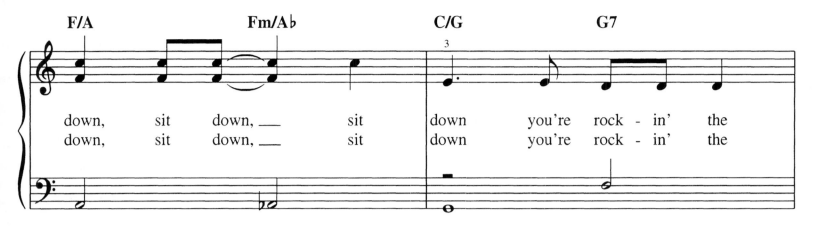

down, sit down, __ sit down you're rock - in' the
down, sit down, __ sit down you're rock - in' the

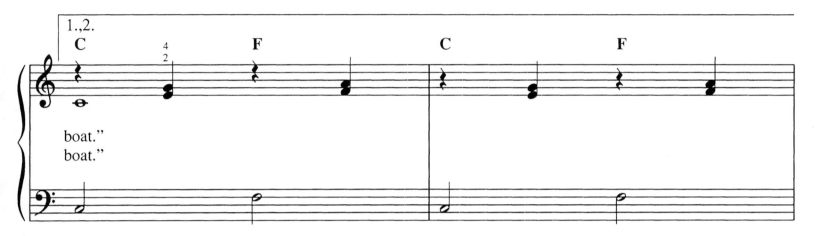

1.,2.

boat."
boat."

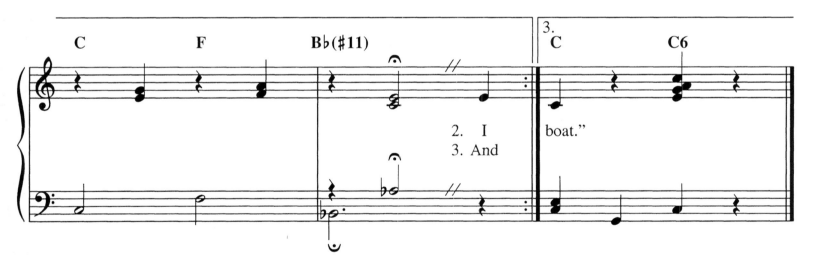

2. I
3. And

boat."

Additional Lyrics

3. And as I laughed at those passengers to Heaven
   A great big wave came and washed me overboard,
   And as I sank, and I hollered, "Someone save me,"
   That's the moment I woke up, thank the Lord.

   And I said to myself, "Sit down, sit down you're rockin' the boat."
   Said to myself, "Sit down, sit down you're rockin' the boat.
   And the devil will drag you under
   With a soul so heavy you'd never float.
   Sit down, sit down, sit down, sit down,
   Sit down, you're rockin' the boat."

VOCAL SELECTIONS FROM THESE *Frank Loesser* SCORES

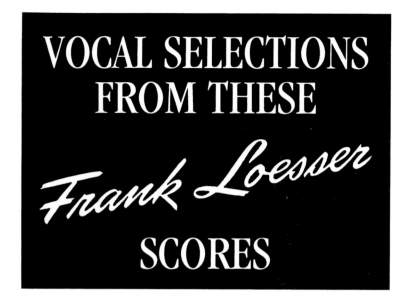

Hans Christian Andersen

Anywhere I Wander • The Inch Worm • The King's New Clothes • No Two People • Thumbelina • The Ugly Duckling • Wonderful Copenhagen

THE MOST HAPPY FELLA

Big D • Don't Cry • Joey, Joey, Joey • The Most Happy Fella • My Heart Is So Full Of You • Somebody, Somewhere • Standing On The Corner • Warm All Over

Adelaide's Lament • A Bushel And A Peck • Fugue For Tinhorns • Guys And Dolls • I'll Know • I've Never Been In Love Before • If I Were A Bell • Luck Be A Lady • More I Cannot Wish You • Sit Down You're Rockin' The Boat • Sue Me • Take Back Your Mink

Lovelier Than Ever • Make A Miracle • My Darling, My Darling • The New Ashmolean Marching Society And Students Conservatory Band • Once In Love With Amy • Pernambuco • Where's Charley?

Brotherhood Of Man • Grand Old Ivy • Happy To Keep His Dinner Warm • How To Succeed In Business Without Really Trying • I Believe In You • Love From A Heart Of Gold • Paris Original

THE BEST OF FRANK LOESSER

85 Great Frank Loesser Songs including selections from:

GUYS AND DOLLS • THE MOST HAPPY FELLA • HANS CHRISTIAN ANDERSEN • HOW TO SUCCEED IN BUSINESS WITHOUT REALLY TRYING • WHERE'S CHARLEY? • GREENWILLOW

Vocal Scores available:
**GUYS & DOLLS* • THE MOST HAPPY FELLA* •
HOW TO SUCCEED IN BUSINESS WITHOUT REALLY TRYING • WHERE'S CHARLEY?**
*1992 Broadway cast albums available on RCA Victor.

FRANK MUSIC CORP.

EXCLUSIVELY DISTRIBUTED BY

HAL•LEONARD® CORPORATION
7777 W. BLUEMOUND RD. P.O. BOX 13819 MILWAUKEE, WI 53213

mpl